History Highlights

TIMELINE of the
MIDDLE AGES

By Charlie Samuels

Gareth Stevens
Publishing

Please visit our Web site www.garethstevens.com. For a free color catalog of all our high-quality books, call toll free 1-800-542-2595 or fax 1-877-542-2596.

Library of Congress Cataloging-in-Publication Data
Samuels, Charlie, 1961-
    Timeline of the Middle Ages / Charlie Samuels.
      p. cm. — (History highlights)
    Includes index.
    ISBN 978-1-4339-3483-4 (library binding) — ISBN 978-1-4339-3484-1 (pbk.)
    ISBN 978-1-4339-3485-8 (6-pack)
    1. Middle Ages—Chronology—Juvenile literature. 2. Europe—History—476-1492—Juvenile literature. I. Title.
D118.S29 2010
940.102'02—dc22
2009037152

Published in 2010 by
Gareth Stevens Publishing
111 East 14th Street, Suite 349
New York, NY 10003

© 2010 The Brown Reference Group Ltd.

For Gareth Stevens Publishing:
Art Direction: Haley Harasymiw
Editorial Direction: Kerri O'Donnell

For The Brown Reference Group Ltd:
Editorial Director: Lindsey Lowe
Managing Editor: Tim Cooke
Editor: Ben Hollingum
Children's Publisher: Anne O'Daly
Design Manager: David Poole
Designer: Karen Perry
Picture Manager: Sophie Mortimer
Production Director: Alastair Gourlay

Picture Credits:
Front Cover: Topfoto: The Granger Collection:

Corbis: Bettmann: 38; The Gallery Collection: 36, 40t; The Picture Desk: 10, 13, 32, 41; istockphoto: Artiva 26r; Jupiter Images: Photos.com: 5, 11, 12c, 14, 28, 33t, 35t, 45; Stockxpert: 6l, 7, 9, 16, 18, 21t, 24, 3142; Shutterstock: Dave Coadwell: 23r; Lucertolone 27; Sergey Vasilyev: 26l; Wikipedia: 39

All Artworks Brown Reference Group

Publisher's note to educators and parents: Our editors have carefully reviewed the Web sites that appear on p. 47 to ensure that they are suitable for students. Many Web sites change frequently, however, and we cannot guarantee that a site's future contents will continue to meet our high standards of quality and educational value. Be advised that students should be closely supervised whenever they access the Internet.

Manufactured in the United States of America
1 2 3 4 5 6 7 8 9 12 11 10

CPSIA compliance information: Batch #BRW0102GS: For further information contact Gareth Stevens, New York, New York at 1-800-542-2595.

Contents

Introduction

Medieval Europe was a continent of contrasts: in many ways life was hard and violent, yet Europeans achieved remarkable advances in culture and commerce.

The Middle Ages are a difficult period to define precisely. In many ways, they were a continuation of what had gone before. Advances in learning and the arts, meanwhile, paved the way for the Renaissance, which began in the fifteenth century. However, the Middle Ages were a time of great social and cultural upheaval and achievement, which formed the basis for the emergence of the early modern world.

Not Such a Dark Age

Historians often date the start of the Middle Ages to 476, when the last Roman emperor in the west was deposed by a barbarian chief. After the fall of Rome, Europe was ruled by what the Romans had called "barbarian" peoples. This was the period once known as the "Dark Ages," yet in many ways society and culture thrived. Rulers such as Charlemagne developed systems of government that were early versions of modern countries. They celebrated their Christian beliefs with huge cathedrals and other works of art. Thinkers explored the meaning of faith, while monasteries became dynamic cultural centers. Trade increased and led to the creation of a more urban society as people moved into towns. Ideas moved with goods along trade routes that ran east to the Muslim world and as far as China.

About This Book

This book focuses on the early Middle Ages, from about 500 to 1300. It contains two different types of timelines. Along the bottom of the pages is a timeline that covers the whole period. It lists key events and developments, color-coded by region. Each chapter also has its own timeline, running vertically down the sides of the pages. This timeline provides more specific details about the particular subject of the chapter.

The Middle Ages are remembered as a time of instability, when society retreated to fortified towns and castles. ⭳

The Byzantine Empire

The Byzantine Empire developed from the eastern Roman Empire but was heavily influenced by Greek and West Asian culture.

The sixth-century Hagia (Saint) Sophia was the largest church in the world until 1547. Today it has been turned into a mosque. ⇒

The Emperor Justinian holds a golden bowl in this mosaic from the Church of San Vitale in Ravenna, Italy. ⬇

TIMELINE
500–540

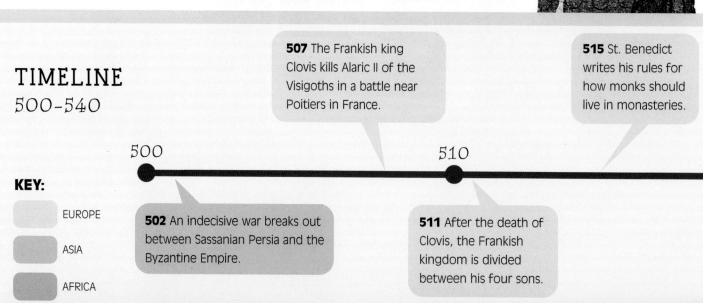

507 The Frankish king Clovis kills Alaric II of the Visigoths in a battle near Poitiers in France.

515 St. Benedict writes his rules for how monks should live in monasteries.

500

510

502 An indecisive war breaks out between Sassanian Persia and the Byzantine Empire.

511 After the death of Clovis, the Frankish kingdom is divided between his four sons.

KEY:

EUROPE

ASIA

AFRICA

Byzantium's first great emperor was also the last truly Roman ruler. Justinian I, who came to the throne in 527, tried to restore imperial rule in the west. His general Belisarius won back North Africa from the Vandals and fought for 20 years to drive the Ostrogoths from Italy.

Barbarian Invasion

Justinian's gains did not last. After his death, the Lombards—a "barbarian" people—conquered northern Italy. Avars, Bulgars, and Slavs drove the population out of much of the Balkans. Persian armies reached Constantinople in 609 and 625. Fighting to survive, the empire grew less concerned with the west. Greek replaced Latin as the official language.

In 627 the Emperor Heraclius crushed the Persians, but soon faced an even stronger enemy. Arabs inspired by the new religion of Islam seized Palestine, Syria, and Egypt from the Byzantines. They might have

Timeline of the Byzantine Empire

529 Justinian I codifies Roman law.

534 Belisarius takes North Africa from the Vandals in the first part of a campaign to restore the western empire.

568 Lombards occupy Italy north of the Po River.

572 Warfare begins again between Byzantium and Persia.

626 Constantinople survives a siege by an alliance of Persians, Slavs, and Avars; in 627 the Byzantines defeat the Persians at Nineveh.

637 The Arabs conquer Mesopotamia, Syria, and (in 639) Egypt.

← This mosaic of Jesus Christ is typical of the Byzantine artistic style.

529 St. Benedict founds the monastery at Monte Cassino in Italy.

c.537 King Arthur, the semilegendary king of the Britons, is killed fighting Saxon invaders.

530

540

523 The Roman philosopher Boethius writes *The Consolation of Philosophy*. It is widely read for over 1,000 years.

c.537 The Emperor Justinian closes the temple of Philae on the Nile, marking the end of the worship of ancient Egyptian gods.

538 The church of St. Sophia is consecrated in Constantinople. It remains the largest church in the Christian world for 1,000 years.

Timeline (continued)

726 Leo III bans the worship of icons, sparking a controversy that lasts until 843.

860 Varangians—Vikings from Russia—attack Constantinople.

867 Basil I establishes the Macedonian Dynasty.

880 Basil I reconquers Calabria (in southern Italy) from the Arabs.

988 Basil II makes an alliance with Vladimir, prince of Kiev, who marries Basil's sister and converts to Orthodox Christianity.

1453 The Byzantine Empire ends when Constantinople falls to the Ottoman Turks.

The Byzantine Empire began as the eastern half of the Roman Empire. →

taken Constantinople itself but for the Byzantine navy and its secret weapon, "Greek fire"—an inflammable substance that was pumped over enemy ships.

The Iconoclasts

Wars with the Arabs helped cause a serious rift between the Orthodox ("right-believing") and Roman Catholic churches. Emperor Leo III thought the Muslims' military success was based on their ban on religious

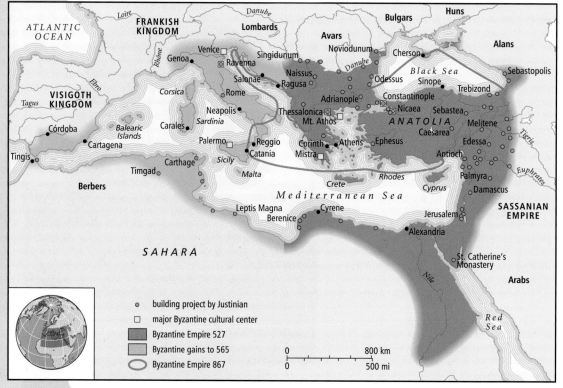

- ● building project by Justinian
- □ major Byzantine cultural center
- Byzantine Empire 527
- Byzantine gains to 565
- ⬭ Byzantine Empire 867

0   800 km
0   500 mi

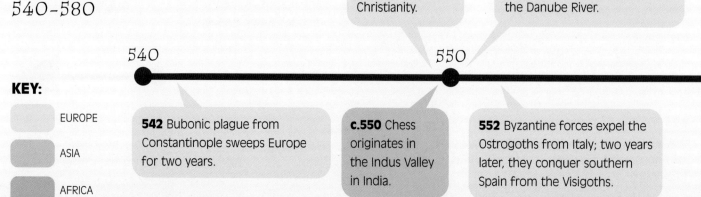

TIMELINE
540–580

540

550

c.550 St. David begins converting the Welsh to Christianity.

c.550 The farming Slav peoples, probably from Belarus and Ukraine, move south across the Danube River.

KEY:

EUROPE

ASIA

AFRICA

542 Bubonic plague from Constantinople sweeps Europe for two years.

c.550 Chess originates in the Indus Valley in India.

552 Byzantine forces expel the Ostrogoths from Italy; two years later, they conquer southern Spain from the Visigoths.

images. In 726, he ordered the destruction of religious pictures and statues. When news reached the pope, he called Leo a heretic. The use of religious icons was restored in Byzantium in 843. By then the gulf with Rome was too wide to be bridged.

Golden Age

In response to the Arab threat, the Byzantines organized their territory into military districts, or *themes*. The system worked, and Byzantium enjoyed a golden age under the Macedonian Dynasty founded in 867. But the *themes* also laid the foundation for the emergence of landed families. These nobles competed for imperial power in the 11th century, when Byzantium faced new threats from Normans in the west and Turks in the east. Even so, the empire survived in a shrunken form until 1453, when its capital Constantinople finally fell to the Ottoman Turks.

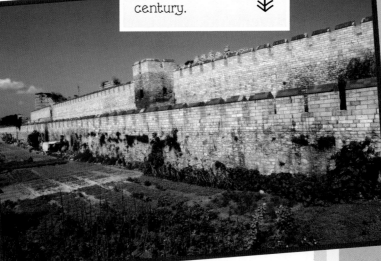

On its landward side, Constantinople was protected by massive walls built in the fifth century. ⇊

Constantinople

Constantinople was a meeting place for major trade routes. That helped make it the largest city in Europe. Controlling the seaway between the Black Sea and the Aegean, it also had a harbor in an inlet called the Golden Horn. The hub of the city was the Hippodrome, which staged chariot races and theatrical performances. The city was also home to magnificent palaces, monuments, and churches.

569 The Byzantines defeat an army of Slavs and Huns at Constantinople.

572 The Byzantine Emperor Justin renews war against the Sassanians.

c.580 Avars, originally from Central Asia, invade the Balkans and threaten the Byzantine Empire.

570

580

562 The Treaty of Edessa brings peace between the Byzantine Empire and Sassanian Persia.

c.570 The Prophet Muhammad, founder of Islam, is born in Mecca in Arabia.

574 Khusrow I of Persia conquers Yemen and makes it part of the Sassanian Empire.

The Frankish Kingdom

After the Roman Empire collapsed, the Frankish king Clovis and his successors built a kingdom in what are now France, Switzerland, and part of western Germany.

King Pepin is crowned king of the Franks by the Pope in 754. →

TIMELINE
580–620

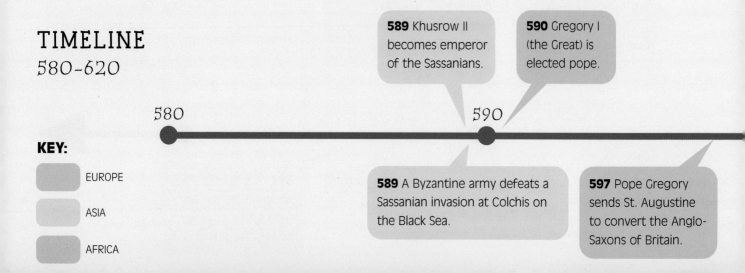

589 Khusrow II becomes emperor of the Sassanians.

590 Gregory I (the Great) is elected pope.

580

590

589 A Byzantine army defeats a Sassanian invasion at Colchis on the Black Sea.

597 Pope Gregory sends St. Augustine to convert the Anglo-Saxons of Britain.

KEY:

EUROPE

ASIA

AFRICA

The early Frankish kings belonged to the Merovingian Dynasty, named for an ancestor called Meroweg. The Frankish churchman Gregory of Tours (c.538–594), who wrote a history of the Merovingians, reported that they were known as "the long-haired kings" because they grew their hair over their shoulders. At the time, long hair and beards were considered signs of a barbarian. The citizens of Gaul were influenced by the Romans: they were clean-shaven and their hair was short.

Clovis Leads the Merovingians

The Merovingians took on the customs of their Gallic subjects. In 491, for example, Clovis was baptized as a Catholic. This was probably a political move rather than a religious conversion: to rule his new lands effectively, Clovis needed to have the church on his side, since bishops helped run local affairs.

CLOVIS. I.

⤆ Like the other Merovingians, Clovis had long hair that came down over his collar.

Timeline of the Frankish Kingdom

481 Clovis becomes king of the Franks, whose territory lies in present-day Belgium.

507 Clovis drives the Visigoths from Aquitaine (southwest France).

511 Clovis dies; his kingdom is divided among his four sons.

536 Burgundy (eastern France and Switzerland) becomes part of the Frankish Kingdom.

537 The Franks win control of Provence (southeastern France).

613 Lothair II reunites the Frankish Kingdom.

638 Dagobert I, last of the great Merovingian kings, dies.

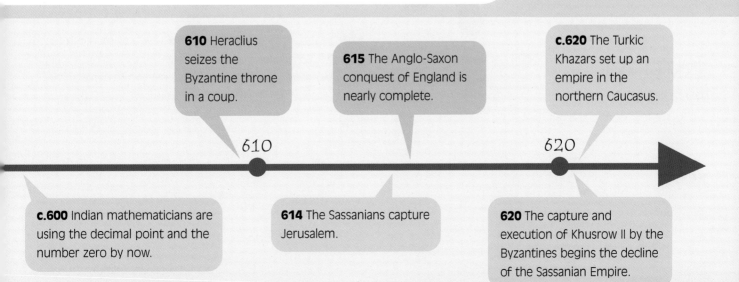

610 Heraclius seizes the Byzantine throne in a coup.

615 The Anglo-Saxon conquest of England is nearly complete.

c.620 The Turkic Khazars set up an empire in the northern Caucasus.

610

620

c.600 Indian mathematicians are using the decimal point and the number zero by now.

614 The Sassanians capture Jerusalem.

620 The capture and execution of Khusrow II by the Byzantines begins the decline of the Sassanian Empire.

Timeline (continued)

687 Pepin of Héristal, mayor of the palace, unites the Frankish territories at the Battle of Tertry.

714 Charles Martel succeeds his father Pepin as mayor of the palace and effective ruler of the Franks.

732 Charles Martel wins a decisive victory over an Arab army at Tours.

741 Charles Martel dies and is succeeded by his son Pepin.

754 Pepin is crowned by the pope in a ceremony at Reims, northern France, that formally affirms the Carolingian dynasty as kings of the Franks.

Charles Martel got his nickname of "Hammer" for his defeat of an Arab army at Tours. ⇒

The Frankish Kingdom was largely the creation of Clovis, greatest of the Merovingian kings. ⇒

✕ major battle
⟶ campaign by Clovis
▉ Frankish territory on accession of Clovis
▉ gains to Frankish Kingdom by Clovis
▉ gains by Clovis's sons to 561

North Sea   Frisians   Saxons   *Elbe*
Tournai • Cologne •   Thuringians
Cambrai • AUSTRASIA   Aix •
Rouen •   Soissons   Trier •   • Worms   *Danube*
486 ✕   Verdun •
Paris •   *Seine*   • Strasbourg   Bavarians
Bretons   NEUSTRIA   Alemanni
Le Mans •   Orléans •   Salzburg •
Tours • *Loire*   FRANKISH KINGDOM
Vouillé ✕   Autun ✕
507 • Poitiers   532   BURGUNDY
ATLANTIC OCEAN   Lyon • A L P S   OSTROGOTH KINGDOM
Bordeaux •   AQUITAINE   Milan •   *Po*
Garonne   Genoa •
GASCONY   • Toulouse   Arles • PROVENCE
Basques   Narbonne •   • Marseille
P Y R E N E E S   *Rhône*   *Mediterranean Sea*   Corsica
VISIGOTH KINGDOM   *Ebro* Zaragoza •   300 km / 200 mi
Barcelona •

When Clovis died in his new capital of Paris in 511, his kingdom was divided between his four sons in accordance with Frankish tribal law. For most of the next 200 years, the Frankish lands were separated into distinct kingdoms. They were only rarely united under a single king. Rival heirs were constantly at war with one another, and assassinations were frequent. Real power passed from these *rois faineants* ("do-nothing kings") to the stewards of

TIMELINE
620–660

626 Constantinople resists a siege by Avars, Slavs, and Persians.

629 Byzantine conquests in Egypt, Syria, and Palestine soon face a new threat from Arab Muslims.

632 Death of Muhammad; Arab forces begin campaigns against the Sassanians and Byzantines. In 638 they capture Jerusalem.

620 ●――――――――――――――――――――――――――――― 630

622 Muhammad and his followers flee from Mecca to Medina; this *hijra* marks the start of the Muslim calendar.

627 The Byzantines defeat the Sassanians at Nineveh.

c.630 East Anglia dominates the seven Anglo-Saxon kingdoms of England.

KEY:

▉ EUROPE

▉ ASIA

▉ AFRICA

the royal household, officials who were known as "mayors of the palace."

By the mid-seventh century, the mayors of the palace were drawn exclusively from the Carolingian family (their name comes from *Carolus*, the Latin form of Charles).

The Hammer

The most outstanding Carolingian mayor was Charles Martel ("the Hammer"). He earned his nickname after a victory over an Arab army near Tours in 732 that stopped the Islamic advance into Christian Europe. Charles Martel helped the mission of St. Boniface to convert the Germans to Christianity and was a great supporter of the church. He was succeeded by his son Pepin the Short. In 751 Pepin got permission from the pope to depose the reigning Merovingian king. He got an assembly of Frankish nobles to elect him king instead as the first ruler of a new Carolingian line.

↑ Kings funded household forces like this Lombard cavalryman.

Warrior Kings

After the fall of the Roman Empire, local kings tried to keep order, but for most people life was more dangerous without Roman armies to keep the peace. Kings fought rivals and stayed in power through military success. They maintained groups of fighting men in their households at their own expense. It was from these household soldiers that the knights of medieval Europe would develop.

645 The Umayyad caliphs set up their capital at Damascus in modern-day Syria.

c.650 Visigoth rule in Spain is weakened by quarreling factions.

650

660

641 The Emperor Heraclius dies, leaving the Byzantine Empire facing enemies on all sides.

654 Arab forces march into the heart of the Byzantine Empire in Anatolia.

656 A civil war over the succession to the Prophet Muhammad divides Islam.

The Emperor Charlemagne

The most famous Carolingian was Charlemagne, literally "Charles the Great." During his reign (768–814), he more than doubled the territory of the Franks.

Charlemagne set out to revive the glory of the Roman Empire. ⬇

This thirteenth-century stained glass window from France shows Charlemagne (center) being crowned by the pope (right). ⇒

TIMELINE
660–700

661 Ali, the son-in-law of Muhammad, is murdered; Islam splits into Shiite and Sunni branches.

678 Byzantine forces use "Greek fire" to end a five-year blockade of Constantinople by the Muslims.

660

670

KEY:

EUROPE

ASIA

AFRICA

664 The Synod of Whitby establishes the pope's authority over the church in England.

664 The Arab advance into Central Asia reaches Kabul in what is now Afghanistan.

670 Arab armies enter what is now Tunisia and begin a campaign for western North Africa.

According to Einhard, who wrote a life of the
emperor, Charlemagne was an outstanding figure
who always wore the Frankish costume of tunic and

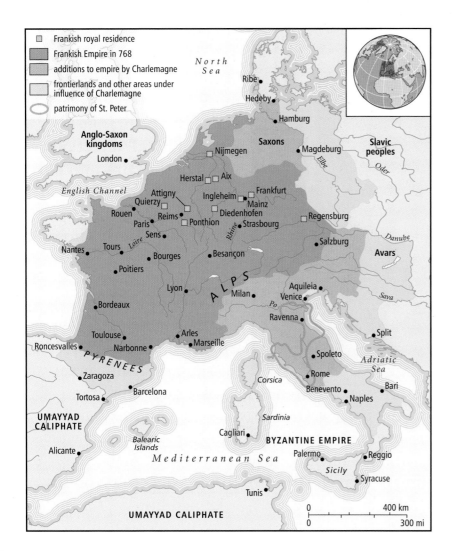

768 Charlemagne succeeds his
father Pepin the Short as king
of the Franks, ruling with his
brother Carloman.

771 Carloman dies;
Charlemagne becomes
sole ruler.

774 Charlemagne visits Rome
for the first time.

781 The pope crowns
Charlemagne's son Pepin as
king of Italy.

782 The Anglo-Saxon scholar
Alcuin, born in York, moves to
the court of Charlemagne.

785 Charlemagne subdues
Saxony after a long campaign;
he begins the conversion of
the Saxons to Christianity.

« Charlemagne's
campaigns extended the
Frankish empire in all
directions.

685 A treaty establishes
a firm frontier between
the Byzantine and
Arab worlds.

687 Venetians make
Venice a republic
with an elected
"doge," or leader.

c.690 English missionaries
preach Christianity in the
Low Countries.

690

700

681 Bulgars agree to protect
Constantinople from Slavic raiders.
In return, the Byzantines recognize
the new Kingdom of Bulgaria.

692 The Sunni Umayyads are
victorious in a second civil war in
Islam.

Timeline (continued)

788 The duke of Bavaria becomes a vassal of Charlemagne.

799 Riots force the pope from Rome; he stays with Charlemagne until restored by Frankish troops.

800 The pope crowns Charlemagne Holy Roman Emperor.

801 Frankish troops capture Barcelona from the Arabs.

812 The Byzantine emperor Michael I recognizes Charlemagne's title.

814 Charlemagne dies; he is succeeded by his son, Louis the Pious.

843 Charlemagne's heirs divide his empire among themselves into three parts at the Treaty of Verdun.

← Charlemagne sits beneath the flag of the European Union.

leggings. Six feet (1.8 m) tall, he had boundless energy and was rarely out of the saddle for long. In more than 50 campaigns, he extended the Frankish kingdom in all directions: south of the Alps into Italy; east to Saxony in Germany; westward into Brittany, France; and south across the Pyrenees into Spain.

Crowned by the Pope

Charlemagne was a devout Christian. He encouraged missionaries, built many monasteries and churches, and gave generous grants of land to the papacy. On Christmas Day in the year 800, when he was on his fifth visit to Rome, Charlemagne attended mass in the Church of St. Peter. As he was kneeling in prayer, Pope Leo III placed a crown on his head, and the congregation acclaimed him as "Caesar" and "Augustus." By this act—which was probably

TIMELINE
700–740

c.700 Avars and Slavs overrun the Balkan peninsula.

718 A Christian army defeats the Arabs in Asturias in northern Spain.

700

710

711 An Arab army invades Spain and advances as far as the Pyrenees Mountains, on the border with France.

719 Pope Gregory II sends St. Boniface to convert the Germans to Christianity.

KEY:

EUROPE

ASIA

AFRICA

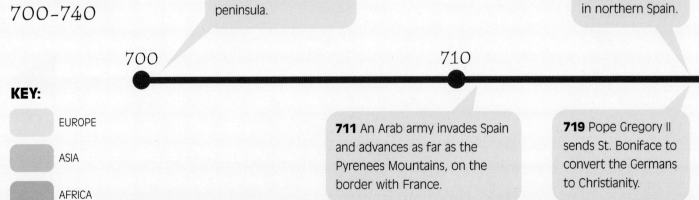

carefully staged with Charlemagne's cooperation—the pope created a Catholic emperor in the west who was independent of the Byzantine ruler in Constantinople. Charlemagne's coronation came to be seen as marking the beginning of the Holy Roman Empire. Under Charlemagne's successors, the Holy Roman Empire survived for another 1,000 years until abolished by the French ruler Napoleon in 1806.

Charlemagne at Peace

When he was not at war, Charlemagne spent his time traveling around his vast territories. He set up court wherever he happened to be. He sent out officials to check on the behavior of local administrators, usually bishops and counts. Although he was probably barely able to read himself, Charlemagne employed the leading scholars of the day, such as Alcuin of York, at his court. He was also a collector of manuscripts. For this reason, his reign is sometimes described as "the Carolingian renaissance." The phrase suggests that Charlemagne oversaw a great revival of learning in Europe.

The Romanesque

Charlemagne is buried in a chapel at Aachen, in Germany. It is built in a style called Romanesque, with round arches and high, small windows. This new style was based on late Roman models. It sent a message that Charlemagne was the successor of the Caesars and had restored the glories of the Roman age.

← The chapel at Aachen is decorated with mosaics.

732 An Arab army from Spain invades France but is defeated at Tours by Franks led by Charles Martel.

739 In Morocco, Berbers and Kharijite Muslims rebel against Arab rule.

730

740

726 A dispute about the use of images in worship—the Iconoclastic Controversy—divides the Orthodox and Roman branches of Christianity.

735 Death of Bede, an Anglo-Saxon monk who has written a history of the church in England.

The Vikings

For many Europeans, the Vikings were heathens and pirates; but the Vikings were also craftsmen, farmers, and traders who helped found the first Russian state.

The shape of a Viking longship struck fear into people along the coasts of Europe. →

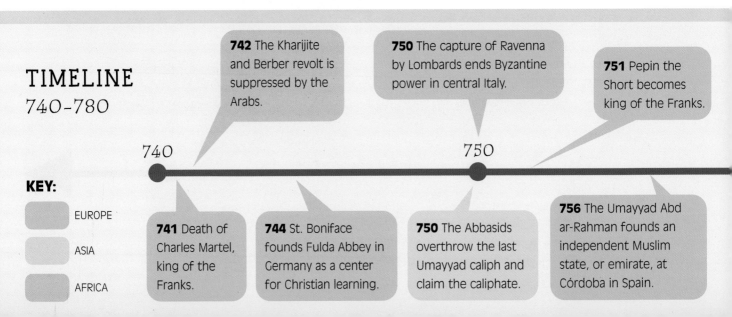

TIMELINE
740–780

742 The Kharijite and Berber revolt is suppressed by the Arabs.

750 The capture of Ravenna by Lombards ends Byzantine power in central Italy.

751 Pepin the Short becomes king of the Franks.

740

750

KEY:

EUROPE

ASIA

AFRICA

741 Death of Charles Martel, king of the Franks.

744 St. Boniface founds Fulda Abbey in Germany as a center for Christian learning.

750 The Abbasids overthrow the last Umayyad caliph and claim the caliphate.

756 The Umayyad Abd ar-Rahman founds an independent Muslim state, or emirate, at Córdoba in Spain.

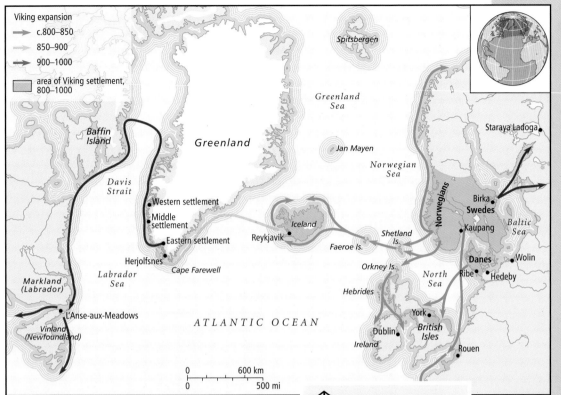

Viking expansion
→ c.800–850
→ 850–900
→ 900–1000
area of Viking settlement, 800–1000

Spitsbergen

Greenland Sea

Baffin Island

Greenland

Jan Mayen

Norwegian Sea

Davis Strait

Western settlement
Middle settlement
Eastern settlement
Herjolfsnes
Cape Farewell

Iceland
Reykjavik
Faeroe Is.
Shetland Is.

Staraya Ladoga

Norwegians

Birka
Swedes
Kaupang
Baltic Sea

Labrador Sea

Markland (Labrador)

L'Anse-aux-Meadows

Vinland (Newfoundland)

Orkney Is.
Hebrides

North Sea

Danes
Ribe
Hedeby
Wolin

ATLANTIC OCEAN

York
Dublin
British Isles
Ireland
Rouen

0   600 km
0   500 mi

↑ By about A.D. 1000, Vikings setting out from Greenland reached the coast of North America, which they called Vinland.

Timeline of the Vikings

c.790 Viking raids on western Europe begin.

793 Vikings raid Lindisfarne Monastery in northern England.

c.830 Viking raids on the English and French coasts increase.

859 Vikings raid Spain and the western Mediterranean.

866 The Danish Great Army lands in England.

867 Danish Vikings in England attack and capture the town of York.

878 Alfred, king of Wessex in southwest England, defeats the Danes at Edington.

882 Oleg makes Kiev capital of the Rus state, which extends from the Gulf of Finland to the Black Sea.

The Vikings were peoples from what are now Norway, Sweden, and Denmark. They shared a common language, religion, and way of life. Originally farmers, they probably left their homes because of a shortage of land. Some settled in uninhabited regions, such as Iceland and Greenland. Others raided settlements elsewhere in Europe for loot. In the tenth

c.760 Arabs start using Indian numerals—the same numbers we use today.

778 The Frankish knight Roland is killed in battle at Roncesvalles; he later becomes the hero of a famous medieval poem, *The Song of Roland*.

770

780

762 Al-Mansur, the Abbasid caliph, sets up his new capital at Baghdad in Iraq.

Timeline (continued)

911 Vikings under Rollo settle in Normandy.

965 Harald Bluetooth of Denmark is baptized as a Christian.

c.986 Vikings settle in Greenland.

c.1000 Viking Greenlanders found a shortlived settlement in Newfoundland.

1016 Cnut (Canute) becomes king of England.

1028 Cnut unites England, Denmark, and Norway in a short-lived North Sea empire.

1085 A large-scale Danish invasion of England is prepared but is abandoned.

Viking ships sailed around the coast of Europe and along the continent's major rivers. ⇒

century, Vikings became the first Europeans known to have landed in North America. They reached Newfoundland, which they called Vinland.

Where the Vikings Settled

Different Viking communities headed to different areas. Norwegian Vikings began to settle in the islands north of Scotland at the beginning of the eighth century. They then moved down the west coast of Britain and across to Ireland, as well as north to Iceland. Danes attacked the western coasts of the European mainland. In the

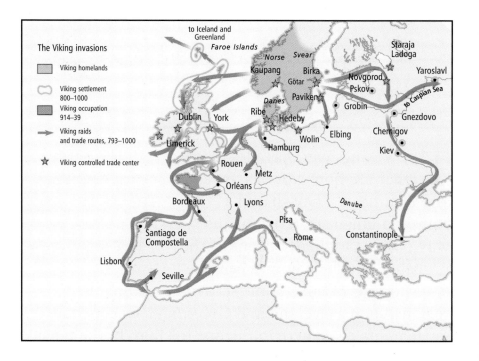

TIMELINE
780–820

786 Harun al-Rashid becomes caliph; he is famed as the ruler of *The Arabian Nights*.

c.790 Irish monks cross the North Atlantic to the Faeroe Islands and Iceland.

791 War breaks out between the Abbasid caliphate and the Byzantine Empire.

780

790

KEY:

EUROPE

ASIA

AFRICA

787 At the Council of Nicaea, the Byzantine Empire orders the worship of images in religious services.

789 The Shiite Idrisids set up their own caliphate in Morocco.

793 Vikings from Scandinavia launch their first major raid, on Holy Island in northeast England.

797 Irene becomes the first empress on the Byzantine throne.

← Holy Island was the first Viking target in England.

mid-ninth century, they invaded England. Eventually they occupied the eastern half of the country, which they ruled as "the Danelaw." Vikings from Sweden moved across the Baltic Sea into eastern Europe. Traveling by river, they eventually reached Constantinople, capital of the Byzantine Empire. They besieged the city unsuccessfully in 860. Many of these eastern Vikings settled in the growing river ports as merchants. The local Slavs called them Rus; they were vital in setting up the first Russian state.

Traders and Raiders

By the ninth century the Viking merchant-warriors had built up a large

Leif Ericson

Leif Ericson (c.970–c.1020) was probably the first European to land in North America. According to Viking sagas, he was the son of the explorer Erik the Red, who settled Greenland. Leif founded a colony in America named Vinland. Archaeologists believe it may have been at L'Anse aux Meadows in Newfoundland.

← The Vikings were fearsome fighters who inspired terror in their opponents.

800 Charlemagne, king of the Franks, is crowned Holy Roman Emperor by the pope.

813 Al-Mamun becomes caliph; his 20-year reign will be celebrated as a highpoint in the history of the caliphate.

817 A treaty brings peace between the Byzantine Empire and the Bulgars of Bulgaria.

810

820

c.800 Arab merchants found trading towns along the East African coast.

814 Charlemagne dies; his throne passes to his son Louis the Pious.

817 Louis the Pious divides the empire among his sons, who agree to rule jointly.

The Longships

The Viking longships marked the most important advance in shipbuilding since the fall of the Roman Empire. First recorded in the late 700s, they carried warriors across western Europe and into the Mediterranean, and also took settlers in stages across the Atlantic to the North American coast. Somtimes the Vikings buried their dead leaders in longships. Several boat graves have been discovered, providing vital information about the vessels.

trading network across the Baltic Sea and Europe. The Vikings supplied timber, furs, and honey in exchange for gold, silver, and luxury goods. Slaves were also an important commodity. The word "slave" stems from the Slav peoples whom the Vikings plundered. Another important source of wealth came in the form of protection money. The Viking raiders had such a fearsome reputation that many western European rulers chose to buy them off. They offered them huge sums of money in return for guarantees of peace.

The longship sat shallow in the water, so it could be rowed up rivers. ⇓

Technological Advances

The entire Viking enterprise was built on technological advances in seamanship. The Norse adventurers were able to cross continents and span seas thanks to their skills in shipbuilding and navigation. Their ships, built with overlapping timber planks, were powered by both sails and oars. The most famous were the longships—fighting vessels holding up to 200 warriors.

TIMELINE
820–860

825 Arabs from Spain conquer Crete.

833 Mojmir founds the kingdom of Moravia.

835 Vikings, mainly Norwegians, begin to settle in Ireland.

820

830

KEY:

EUROPE

ASIA

AFRICA

c.820 Al-Mamun founds the House of Wisdom in Baghdad, an academy for the translation of scientific and philosophical works.

827 The Aghlabids of North Africa conquer the island of Sicily.

836 Caliph Al-Mutasim moves the capital of the caliphate from Baghdad to Samarra.

Viking Navigation

Viking longships made some incredible journeys. Often they sailed within sight of shore, but they also crossed thousands of miles of empty ocean. The magnetic compass, for finding the direction of north, was known in China but not in Europe. Nor had anyone yet worked out how to find longitude (the distances sailed east or west of a certain point). It seems that the Vikings may have invented a navigational instrument that was a cross between a sundial and a compass. Their Sun compass was a wooden disk with 32 notches around the edge corresponding to points of the compass. When the disk was horizontal, a pointed rod or cone at the center cast a shadow. By rotating the disk, the shadow could be made to touch one of two lines scratched on the surface. The lines represented the Sun's apparent path across the heavens, one for the equinoxes and one for the summer solstice. The ship's bearing could then be read off the appropriate notch.

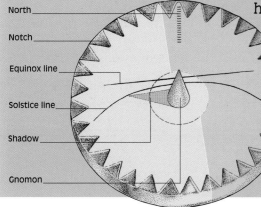

North
Notch
Equinox line
Solstice line
Shadow
Gnomon

King Alfred of Wessex became a British hero for his defeat of the Danes at the Battle of Edington in 878.

837 Jews and Christians in Córdoba, Spain, rebel unsuccessfully against Muslim rule.

843 The Treaty of Verdun breaks up Charlemagne's empire among the three heirs of Louis the Pious.

859 Viking raiders reach the Mediterranean.

850

860

841 Vikings invade Normandy in northern France.

846 An Aghlabid fleet raids Rome.

c.855 Eastern Vikings, known as Varangians or Rus, found the city of Kiev in Ukraine.

The Birth of Russia

Vikings known as Varangians created a pagan state, Rus, between the Baltic and Black seas. Rus traded with the Byzantines, from whom it received the Christian faith.

The Kremlin in Novgorod began as a cathedral built on top of a pagan burial ground in about 989. →

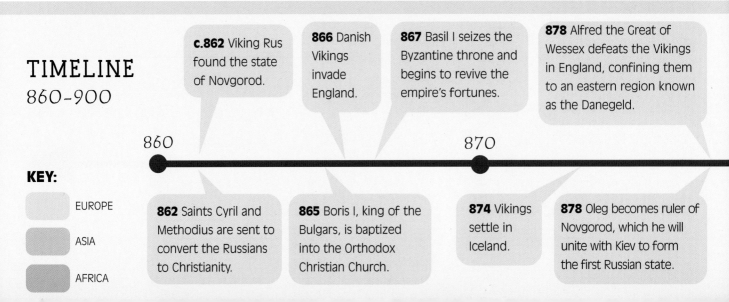

TIMELINE
860-900

KEY:
- EUROPE
- ASIA
- AFRICA

c.862 Viking Rus found the state of Novgorod.

866 Danish Vikings invade England.

867 Basil I seizes the Byzantine throne and begins to revive the empire's fortunes.

878 Alfred the Great of Wessex defeats the Vikings in England, confining them to an eastern region known as the Danegeld.

860

870

862 Saints Cyril and Methodius are sent to convert the Russians to Christianity.

865 Boris I, king of the Bulgars, is baptized into the Orthodox Christian Church.

874 Vikings settle in Iceland.

878 Oleg becomes ruler of Novgorod, which he will unite with Kiev to form the first Russian state.

Russian history traditionally begins in 862, with the founding of Novgorod by a Swedish Viking, or Varangian, called Rurik. But the origins of the state are older. When the Varangians arrived, the area was home to Slavs from the east. The Varangians quickly came to dominate the region and its trade with Constantinople. As well as forest products—furs, timber, and honey—the shipments included captured Slavs, the origin of the word "slave."

According to a Russian chronicle, the Slavs drove out the Varangians in the mid-ninth

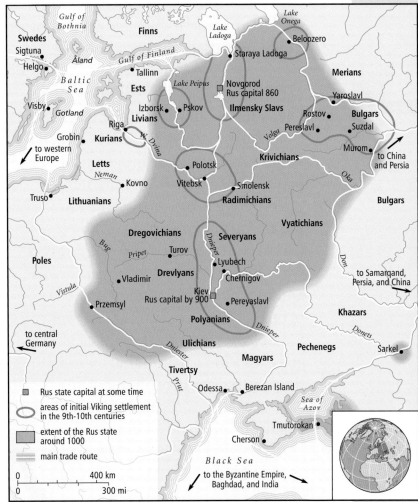

Timeline of Russia

c.500 East Slavs settle along rivers linking the Baltic and Black seas.

c.800 Swedish Vikings or Varangians move into the eastern Slavic lands.

c.862 The Varangian leader Rurik establishes a capital at Novgorod.

882 Rurik's successor, Oleg, makes Kiev capital of the "land of Rus."

c.955 Olga, Igor's widow, joins the Orthodox Church.

962 Sviatoslav, Olga's son, becomes prince of Kiev.

← The Vikings in Russia settled along rivers, which carried trade south to the Black Sea.

c.890 Al-Battani, an Arab astronomer, calculates the exact length of the year.

c.900 The Persian scholar ar-Razi, known in the West as Rhazes, first divides matter into animal, vegetable, or mineral.

890

900

884 Charles the Fat of Germany temporarily reunites Charlemagne's empire.

c.900 The Byzantine Empire begins to revive in Anatolia (modern-day Turkey).

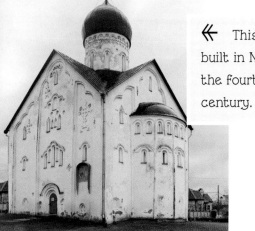

← This church was built in Novgorod in the fourteenth century.

century, but then fell into such disunity that they begged the Vikings to return as rulers. This was when Rurik founded Novgorod, south of present-day St. Petersburg. Twenty years later, Rurik's successor, Oleg, took Kiev and made it the capital of a more southerly kingdom called "the land of Rus."

Trade with Byzantium

Oleg's most famous achievement was an assault on Constantinople with a fleet of 2,000 ships. He won favorable trading privileges from the Byzantines.

Trade with Byzantium brought the pagan Varangians into contact with Christianity. The first royal convert was Olga, widow of a Kievan prince and mother of Sviatoslav, the first prince of Kiev to bear a Slav name. Sviatoslav clung to the old Norse gods, and his pagan beliefs were at first shared by his son Vladimir. Yet in 988, 11 years after gaining the crown, Vladimir ordered the wholesale

This statue celebrates Vladimir, who made Russia Christian. ⇒

Timeline (continued)

965 Sviatoslav briefly occupies the steppes north of the Black Sea, but loses control to the nomadic Pechenegs.

977 Vladimir, a pagan, becomes the new ruler of Rus.

988 Vladimir converts to Orthodox Christianity and has the Russians baptized. In return he marries Anna, sister of the Byzantine emperor.

989 Vladimir sends 6,000 troops to Constantinople; they become famous as the Varangian Guard, the emperor's elite military unit.

TIMELINE
900–940

900 A medical school is founded at Salerno in southern Italy.

c.906 Hungarian Magyars destroy the Slav empire of Moravia.

910 William of Aquitaine founds the Benedictine Abbey of Cluny, Europe's most magnificent monastery.

911 The Byzantines grant trading privileges to Varangian traders from Rus.

900

910

KEY:

EUROPE

ASIA

AFRICA

901 The Saminid dynasty comes to the throne in Persia.

911 The French king makes Rollo, leader of Viking settlers in France, duke of Normandy.

916 Horse-riding Khitan nomads begin a kingdom in Mongolia.

conversion of his people to Christianity.

A Conversion

Legend says that Vladimir chose the Orthodox faith after sending commissioners to study different religions. The men sent to Constantinople described in wonder how, inside the church of St. Sophia, they did not know if they "were on heaven or on earth." In fact, Vladimir's reasons for embracing Orthodox Christianity were political as much as spiritual: His reward for converting was an alliance with Byzantium through marriage to the emperor's sister.

Vladimir's decision had immense consequences. If Russia had converted to Islam, world history would have been incalculably different. At the same time, by embracing the Eastern Orthodox faith rather than Roman Catholicism, Russia was bound to develop along different lines from the rest of Europe.

⚶ Russian Orthodox churches have distinctive onion-shaped domes.

A Wooden City

Medieval Novgorod was built entirely of wood. Its people lived in wooden homes, used wooden drains, prayed in wooden churches, walked on streets surfaced with split logs, and wrote on birch bark. Experts have found more than 1,000 buildings preserved in the damp ground. Digs also turned up many coin hoards, as the Varangians traded furs and other goods for silver dirhams from Central Asia. The dirham, the standard currency in Eastern Europe, became a Viking status symbol.

930 The Althing, the world's oldest parliament, is set up by Viking settlers in Iceland.

935 Arabs found the city of Algiers, in present-day Algeria.

930

940

929 The emir of Córdoba in Spain, Abdurrahman III, proclaims himself caliph, or leader of the Islamic world.

935 Muslim scholars finalize the text of the Koran, the holy book of Islam.

939 Birth of Ferdowsi, who will write Persia's national epic, *Shahnama* ("The Book of Kings").

The Normans

The Normans were the descendants of Vikings who settled in northern France. They carved out an empire that stretched from Britain to the Mediterranean.

King Harold feasts in this tapestry recording the invasion of Britain. →

TIMELINE
940–980

KEY:

EUROPE

ASIA

AFRICA

944 A Viking force attacks London, England.

c.945 Gerbert of Aurillac first uses Hindu-Arabic numbers in Europe—but they do not catch on.

c.950 The Igbo develop an advanced iron-working culture in the Niger Delta.

955 At the Battle of Lechfeld, Germans defeat the Magyars, ending 60 years of Magyar attacks.

940

950

945 An Islamic military group, the Buyids, take power in Baghdad, where they rule in the name of the Abbasids.

947 Khitans from Mongolia establish the Liao dynasty in China, with its capital at Beijing.

954 After the defeat and death of the Viking king Eric Bloodaxe, England is reunited under the Anglo-Saxon king Edred.

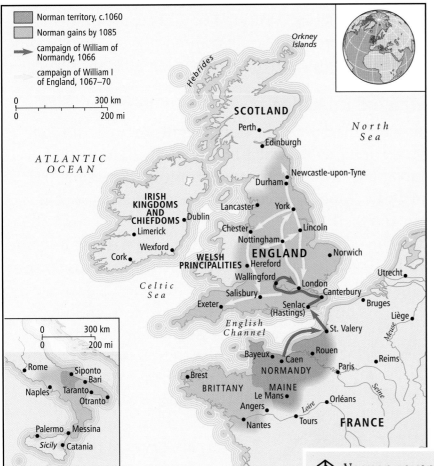

Norman territory, c.1060
Norman gains by 1085
campaign of William of Normandy, 1066
campaign of William I of England, 1067–70

0   300 km
0   200 mi

ATLANTIC OCEAN

Orkney Islands

Hebrides

SCOTLAND

North Sea

Perth
Edinburgh
Newcastle-upon-Tyne
Durham
Lancaster   York
Chester   Lincoln
Nottingham
Norwich
ENGLAND
Hereford
Wallingford   London
Salisbury   Canterbury
Exeter   Senlac (Hastings)
Utrecht
Bruges
Liège
St. Valery
Rouen
Bayeux   Caen
NORMANDY   Paris   Reims
Brest
MAINE
BRITTANY   Le Mans
Angers   Orléans
Nantes   Tours   FRANCE
Seine
Loire
Meuse

IRISH KINGDOMS AND CHIEFDOMS
Dublin
Limerick
Wexford
Cork
Celtic Sea
WELSH PRINCIPALITIES

English Channel

0   300 km
0   200 mi

Rome
Siponto
Bari
Naples   Taranto
Otranto
Palermo   Messina
Sicily   Catania

Timeline of the Normans

911 Rolf, a Viking leader, is granted lands in Normandy.

1013 When Danes invade England, Prince Edward goes into exile in Normandy.

1027 Birth of William, son of Robert, duke of Normandy.

1030 Rainulf becomes the first Norman to gain land in Italy.

1035 William succeeds his father as duke of Normandy.

1042 Edward succeeds to the English throne.

1051 King Edward of England names Duke William as his heir.

1053 The Normans defeat Pope Leo IX at Civitate, Italy.

1060 Norman forces complete the conquest of Calabria and Apulia in Italy.

1061 Normans invade Sicily.

⋔ Norman power spread into Brittany and southern Italy as well as England.

Norman history begins with Rolf, a Viking who in 911 swore homage to the Frankish king in return for land in what was later known as Normandy. Within two generations the Normans adopted the Franks' language, religion, laws,

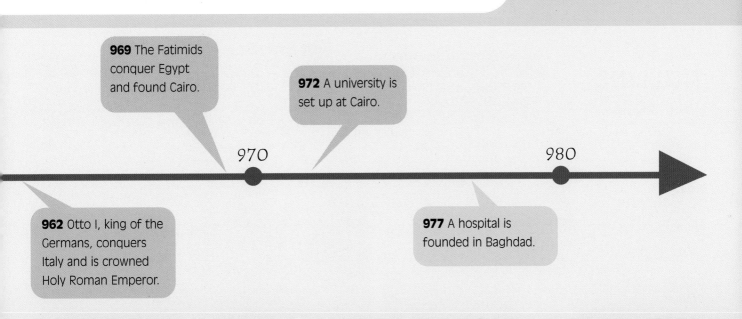

969 The Fatimids conquer Egypt and found Cairo.

972 A university is set up at Cairo.

970

980

962 Otto I, king of the Germans, conquers Italy and is crowned Holy Roman Emperor.

977 A hospital is founded in Baghdad.

1066 On the death of King Edward, William invades England, defeats the new king Harold at Hastings, and is crowned king.

1071 The fall of Bari completes the conquest of Italy.

1072 The Normans invade Scotland.

c.1078 The Normans build the White Tower, a fortress that begins the Tower of London.

1086 William commissions the Domesday Book, a survey of England.

1087 William I dies in France.

1091 The Normans complete the conquest of Sicily.

and cavalry tactics. Mounted knights came to form an aristocracy who held lands granted to them by the duke of Normandy in return for providing military service.

Battle of Hastings

Many Norman younger sons sought fortunes abroad. In Italy, feuding between Lombard, Byzantine, and Arab rulers offered rich opportunities. Between 1061 and 1091, three Norman brothers conquered southern Italy and Sicily.

On the other side of Europe, King Edward of England died in 1066. He had promised the throne to his cousin William, duke of Normandy. On his deathbed, however, the English nobles forced him to choose Harold, earl of Wessex, to succeed him. William assembled an invasion force. Harold defeated another rival, King Harald Hardrada of Norway, then met the Norman army at Hastings. The battle was in the balance before the Normans finally triumphed. Harold died,

⇐ At Hastings, the Normans fought on horseback.

TIMELINE
980–1020

KEY:

EUROPE

ASIA

AFRICA

c.982 Vikings led by Eric the Red set up a first colony in Greenland.

988 Vladimir of Kiev introduces Eastern Orthodox Christianity to Russia.

1000 Venice defeats pirates to gain control of the Adriatic Sea.

980

990

982 A Slav revolt against the Germans recovers territories east of the Elbe River.

987 France's Capetian dynasty begins with the coronation of Hugh Capet as king.

999 Gerbert of Aurillac becomes the first French pope, with the name Sylvester II.

and with him went the old Anglo-Saxon order; for the next 500 years, England would be linked to France.

William confiscated most of the Anglo-Saxon estates. He kept about a fifth of the land for himself and gave the rest to his barons in return for military service. He also installed French bishops. The Normans did not destroy English identity, however. They retained many Anglo-Saxon institutions. And if the English were forced to become more Norman, the Normans also became more English. Only a century after the Battle of Hastings an official reported that "the peoples have become so mingled that no-one can tell...who is of English and who of Norman descent."

↑ The White Tower was 87 feet (27 m) high with walls up to 10 feet (3 m) thick.

Norman Castles

To secure his grip on England, William built castles. The first ones were made of wood with a central tower, or "keep," and a "bailey," or courtyard. The lord's family lived in the keep; his followers lived in the bailey, which had a hall, a chapel, shelter for livestock, and workshops. In the late eleventh century, stone structures appeared. The White Tower—the first Tower of London—is one of the earliest surviving examples.

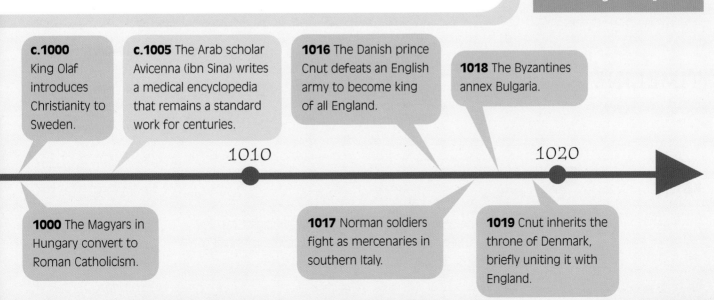

c.1000 King Olaf introduces Christianity to Sweden.

c.1005 The Arab scholar Avicenna (ibn Sina) writes a medical encyclopedia that remains a standard work for centuries.

1016 The Danish prince Cnut defeats an English army to become king of all England.

1018 The Byzantines annex Bulgaria.

1010

1020

1000 The Magyars in Hungary convert to Roman Catholicism.

1017 Norman soldiers fight as mercenaries in southern Italy.

1019 Cnut inherits the throne of Denmark, briefly uniting it with England.

Feudalism

Historians sometimes call the early Middle Ages in Europe—the period from roughly the ninth to the thirteeth century—"the age of feudalism."

Peasants work in the countryside in this illustration from the eleventh century. ⇒

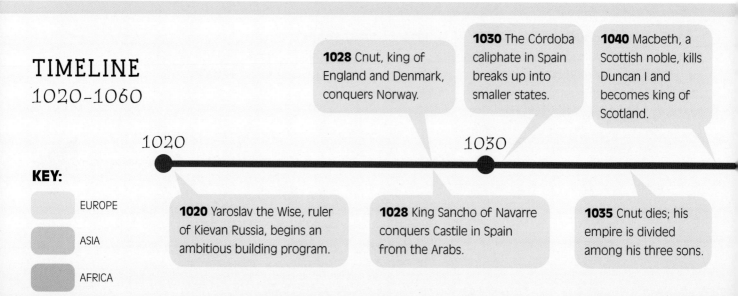

TIMELINE
1020–1060

KEY:

EUROPE

ASIA

AFRICA

1028 Cnut, king of England and Denmark, conquers Norway.

1030 The Córdoba caliphate in Spain breaks up into smaller states.

1040 Macbeth, a Scottish noble, kills Duncan I and becomes king of Scotland.

1020

1030

1020 Yaroslav the Wise, ruler of Kievan Russia, begins an ambitious building program.

1028 King Sancho of Navarre conquers Castile in Spain from the Arabs.

1035 Cnut dies; his empire is divided among his three sons.

Feudalism was a system of contracts by which a king or noble made a grant of land, known as a fief, in return for military service. The beneficiary then swore an oath of loyalty to his lord. In the same way, the peasants who worked the land had an obligation to provide labor for their master in return for the protection he offered, plus a share of the crop.

Rise of the Feudal Lords

Feudalism developed in the territories of western Europe ruled by Charlemagne and his successors in the eighth and ninth centuries. The emperor granted land in return for "knight service,"

meaning that vassals had to send knights (mounted soldiers) to serve in the imperial armies when needed, and to maintain them at their own expense. As feudalism developed,

↑ The wedding of Eleanor of Aquitaine put much French land under English control.

Timeline of Feudalism

843 The Treaty of Verdun states that "every man should have a lord."

911 The Viking leader Rolf does homage to King Charles III of France for lands in Normandy.

c.1095 *The Song of Roland*, an epic poem about a knight, spreads the ideals of chivalry.

1099 Crusader leaders rule the Holy Land as a feudal kingdom divided into four baronies.

c. 1140 Geoffrey of Monmouth's *History of the Kings of Britain* spreads the popular legends of King Arthur and the Round Table.

« In a scene from the Bayeux Tapestry Harold of England swears loyalty to William, duke of Normandy.

1043 Seljuk Turks capture the Persian city of Isfahan.

c.1050 The city of Oslo is founded in Europe.

1054 The split between the Eastern Orthodox and Roman Catholic churches becomes permanent.

1050

1060

1048 The Berber Almoravid clan begin a campaign that will eventually bring them control over much of North Africa.

c.1050 Yaroslav the Wise compiles the first Russian legal code.

1055 Seljuk Turks capture Baghdad from the Buyids and restore the caliphate.

vassals were also expected to provide other duties and services, such as giving advice in the lord's council. In exchange, they received both the income of the land and legal authority over all who lived on it.

Feudal lords lived in castles on estates (manors). Peasants farmed the land and paid part of the harvest to the lord as rent. In return, the lord was expected to protect peasants in times of war and judge any disputes.

By the eleventh and

≪ Feudal Europe was a patchwork of lands owned by the church, by rulers, or by nobles holding royal fiefs.

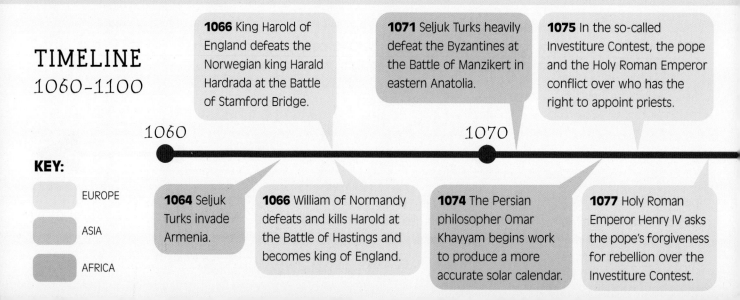

TIMELINE 1060–1100

1066 King Harold of England defeats the Norwegian king Harald Hardrada at the Battle of Stamford Bridge.

1071 Seljuk Turks heavily defeat the Byzantines at the Battle of Manzikert in eastern Anatolia.

1075 In the so-called Investiture Contest, the pope and the Holy Roman Emperor conflict over who has the right to appoint priests.

1060

1070

1064 Seljuk Turks invade Armenia.

1066 William of Normandy defeats and kills Harold at the Battle of Hastings and becomes king of England.

1074 The Persian philosopher Omar Khayyam begins work to produce a more accurate solar calendar.

1077 Holy Roman Emperor Henry IV asks the pope's forgiveness for rebellion over the Investiture Contest.

KEY:

EUROPE

ASIA

AFRICA

← Frederick I ruled the Holy Roman Empire as a feudal system.

twelfth centuries fiefs were hereditary. Some feudal lords ruled vast estates. In France, for example, the royal lands covered a small area around Paris; the lands held by nobles such as the counts of Anjou and Aquitaine were much larger than those of the king.

Lord and Vassal

This imbalance had some odd results. In 1152, Henry of Anjou married Eleanor of Aquitaine, the divorced wife of Louis VII of France and heiress to much of France south of the Loire River. Two years later, Henry became King Henry II of England and duke of Normandy. Yet even though he was now the most powerful ruler in Europe, he tried to avoid open warfare with the French king who was his feudal lord in Aquitaine, since to do so would set a bad example to his own vassals.

Chivalry

By the 12th century, relations between lords and vassals were governed by chivalry (from the French *chevalier*, meaning "knight"). A knight was expected to show honesty, loyalty, courage, and strength. He was bound to obey his lord, protect the church, respect women, and go on crusades. Knights trained by jousting in tournaments. The ideas of chivalry were spread in popular poems and songs.

← Mounted knights had young assistants called squires to help them.

1086 William I of England orders a survey of his realm, recorded in the Domesday Book.

1091 The Norman Roger de Hauteville completes his conquest of Sicily.

1095 The Byzantine emperor appeals to the West for military aid against the Seljuk Turks; Pope Urban II proclaims the First Crusade.

1099 Spanish hero El Cid dies defending Valencia from Muslims.

1090

1100

1083 Henry IV's army captures Rome.

1086 Almoravids from Morocco establish rule over much of Spain.

1092 On the death of Malik Shah, the Seljuk sultanate begins to break up.

1099 After victories at Nicaea and Antioch, crusaders from western Europe conquer Jerusalem.

The Holy Roman Empire

The Holy Roman Empire tried to revive the old Roman Empire in Christian form. Its emperors were overlords of central Europe and north Italy.

This crown was made in the tenth century for Emperor Otto I. ⟫

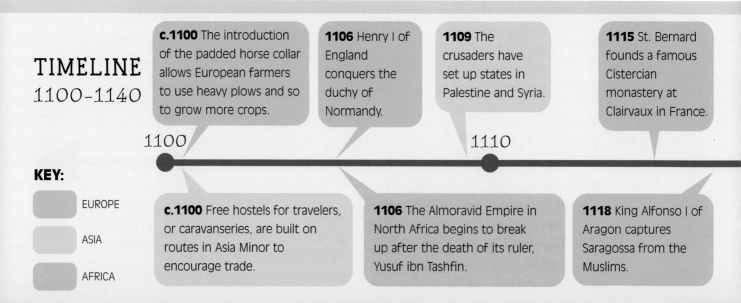

TIMELINE 1100–1140

KEY:
- EUROPE
- ASIA
- AFRICA

c.1100 The introduction of the padded horse collar allows European farmers to use heavy plows and so to grow more crops.

1106 Henry I of England conquers the duchy of Normandy.

1109 The crusaders have set up states in Palestine and Syria.

1115 St. Bernard founds a famous Cistercian monastery at Clairvaux in France.

1100

1110

c.1100 Free hostels for travelers, or caravanseries, are built on routes in Asia Minor to encourage trade.

1106 The Almoravid Empire in North Africa begins to break up after the death of its ruler, Yusuf ibn Tashfin.

1118 King Alfonso I of Aragon captures Saragossa from the Muslims.

The empire had one great flaw. The emperor was the champion of Christendom in the secular world. He had to cooperate with the pope, the spiritual head of the church. In fact, the two leaders were opponents as often as they were allies.

Unlike other rulers of the time, the emperor was elected by nobles of his realm. In practice, great families came to dominate the post. From 1024 to 1125, the Salian family provided a succession of

From 1194, the northern empire was added to by the Kingdom of Sicily, which included Sicily and southern Italy. →

main Hohenstaufen palace or castle

seat of archbishop within the Holy Roman Empire

Holy Roman Empire under the Hohenstaufen, c.1254

territory in Italy claimed by the pope

0   400 km
0   300 mi

Timeline of the Holy Roman Empire

800 Charlemagne, king of the Franks, is crowned as the first Holy Roman Emperor.

1075 Pope Gregory VII declares it illegal for non-churchmen to appoint bishops, starting the Investiture Contest.

1076 At the Synod of Worms, bishops loyal to Henry IV declare Pope Gregory deposed; Gregory excommunicates Henry.

1077 Threatened by rebellion, Henry goes to Italy to ask Gregory's forgiveness.

1122 The Concordat of Worms ends the Investiture Contest.

1138 Conrad III is the first Hohenstaufen emperor.

1122 The Concordat of Worms ends the Investiture Contest between the pope and Holy Roman Emperor.

c.1125 Monks from new Cistercian abbeys clear land and improve agriculture across western Europe.

1137 Eleanor of Aquitaine marries King Louis VII of France.

1130

1140

1124 The capture of Tyre means that most of Palestine is now part of the Latin Kingdom of Palestine.

c.1136 The church of St. Denis near Paris introduces the Gothic style of architecture.

1138 Conrad III of the Hohenstaufen family becomes German emperor.

Timeline (continued)

1152 Frederick I (Barbarossa) succeeds to the throne.

1176 Frederick is defeated by the Lombard League of Italian cities at Legnano.

1183 Frederick acknowledges the Italian cities' right to govern themselves.

1197 The death of Henry VI begins 14 years of civil war in Germany.

1220 Frederick II of Germany becomes emperor.

1237 Frederick defeats the Lombard League at the Battle of Cortenuova.

1238 The excommunication of Frederick begins a 12-year war between the emperor and an alliance of the papacy and the Italian cities.

1250 Frederick dies with the struggle unresolved.

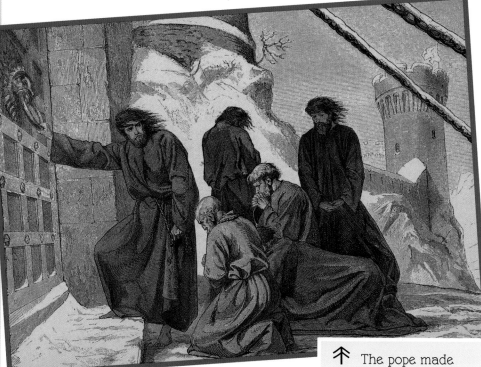

↑ The pope made Henry IV wait three days in the snow to ask for forgiveness.

emperors. When the last Salian ruler died heirless, the electors chose as his successor Lothair II, a member of the powerful Welf clan, over a candidate from the Hohenstaufen family. That began one of the great dynastic rivalries of the Middle Ages, as lesser lords sided with either Welfs or Waiblingers—an alternative name for the Hohenstaufens, from their castle of Waiblingen in Germany. In Italy, the names became corrupted into Guelphs and Ghibellines. The

TIMELINE 1140–1180

1146 The Second Crusade is launched after Muslim victories against the Latin kingdoms of the Holy Land.

1150 Eric "the Saint" becomes king of Sweden and begins to convert the Finns to Christianity.

c.1150 The Seljuk sultanate of Rum occupies much former Byzantine territory in Anatolia.

1154 Henry of Anjou inherits the English crown as King Henry II, founding the Plantagenet dynasty.

1140   1150

KEY:

EUROPE

ASIA

AFRICA

1143 Afonso Henriques wins independence from the Spanish kingdom of León and is crowned the first king of Portugal.

1147 The Almohads replace the Almoravids as the chief power in North Africa.

c.1150 A university is founded in Paris.

1159 Frederick I Barbarossa sets up an "antipope" to oppose the power of the Vatican.

two groups divided the northern cities at the start of the Renaissance.

However bitter the divisions separating rival claimants to the title, an even bigger gulf opened between emperor and pope. The two first fell out in the eleventh-century Investiture Contest. Strife was renewed in the twelfth century, when the Hohenstaufen family finally established itself on the imperial throne. One of the greatest Hohenstaufens, Frederick I, known as Barbarossa ("Red Beard"), tried to impose his authority on the papacy and the northern Italian cities by military means. He was defeated by their combined forces at the Battle of Legnano in 1176.

War Between Pope and Emperor

Even worse divisions emerged in the 38-year reign of Frederick II. Known as Stupor Mundi ("The World's Wonder"), Frederick was a brilliant, ruthless ruler. By dynastic chance, he inherited the Kingdom of Sicily, made up not just of Sicily but also of southern Italy, as well as the imperial title. His lands sandwiched the pope's central Italian

This monument honors a warrior of the Lombard ⇓ League.

Origins of the Empire

The origin of the Holy Roman Empire is usually traced back to the coronation of Charlemagne in 800. When Charlemagne's empire was divided after his death, the succession passed to the rulers of its central lands, which included much of Germany and northern Italy. The arrangement encouraged close relations between the rulers of the empire and the popes, for whom the emperors were seen as secular champions.

1172 Knights loyal to Henry II of England kill Thomas Becket, archbishop of Canterbury.

1176 The merchant cities of northern Italy win the Battle of Legnano to remain independent of the Holy Roman Empire.

1180 Stephen Nemanja begins a monarchy in Serbia.

1170

1180

1167 The Christian kingdom of Jerusalem captures Cairo, but it is recaptured by Arabs a year later.

1174 Saladin, the first Ayyubid sultan of Egypt, conquers Syria from the crusaders.

1180 Saladin agrees a truce with the Latin kingdom of Jerusalem.

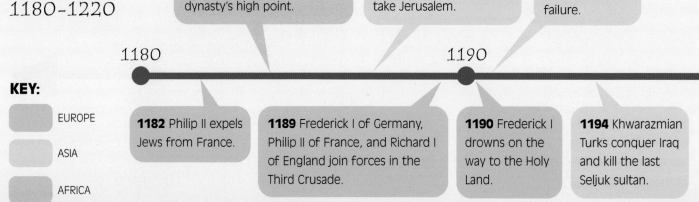

↑ Gregory VII's attempt to assert the power of the papacy began the Investiture Contest.

Emperor Frederick Barbarossa drowned on his way to the crusades. ⇒

The Investiture Contest

In 1075, a reform-minded pope, Gregory VII, decided to insist on his right to invest (appoint) bishops. Because the church controlled great wealth, choosing its leaders was politically important. The emperors wanted to choose bishops themselves. The result was a bitter struggle during which Gregory declared Emperor Henry IV excommunicated (banned from the church). In order to avoid rebellion at home, Henry was forced to seek the pope's forgiveness. But that did not deter him from later declaring all-out war on the pope. The issue continued to trouble later popes and emperors until a compromise solution was finally worked out in 1122. According to the Concordat of Worms (a German city), the pope had the right to appoint bishops but his nominees had to have imperial approval.

TIMELINE
1180–1220

1184 Yaqub al-Mansur comes to the Almohad throne in North Africa, marking the dynasty's high point.

1187 Saladin defeats the crusaders at the Battle of Hattin, then advances to take Jerusalem.

1191 The Third Crusade ends in failure.

1180

1190

KEY:

EUROPE

ASIA

AFRICA

1182 Philip II expels Jews from France.

1189 Frederick I of Germany, Philip II of France, and Richard I of England join forces in the Third Crusade.

1190 Frederick I drowns on the way to the Holy Land.

1194 Khwarazmian Turks conquer Iraq and kill the last Seljuk sultan.

possessions. When Frederick sought to impose his will
on the pope, a bitter 12-year war broke out. The
emperor was repeatedly excommunicated (banned from
the church). In return, Frederick
ravaged the papal lands and sought
to depose the pope.

Weak Empire

Frederick died in 1250
with the struggle
unresolved. The empire
itself outlived the
conflict for many
centuries. It was finally
abolished by the French
emperor Napoleon only
in 1806. Yet its position
as a supporter of the
Christian faith was
fatally weakened. The
real loser in the conflict
was Christendom itself.
It saw the positive energy
unleashed in the
Crusades lost in internal
strife and struggles
among dynasties.

Devils crown the
antipope Clement III
in this cartoon. ⤋

The Antipopes

In the eleventh and
twelfth centuries,
the Holy Roman
Emperors attempted
to limit papal
power by
declaring their
own popes.
These so-called
antipopes sat in
opposition to
the pope in
Rome. The
antipope
Clement III, for
example, was
made pope by
Henry IV during
the Investiture
Contest. The
antipopes never
won popular
support outside
the realms of
the emperors
who supported
them.

c.1200 The Great
Enclosure is built
at Great Zimbabwe
in southern Africa.

1209 Pope Innocent III sends
a crusader army into
southern France to suppress
the Albigensian sect.

1215 King John of England
is forced by nobles to
sign Magna Carta, limiting
royal power.

1210

1220

1204 The forces of the
Fourth Crusade capture
Constantinople; the Byzantine
emperor Alexius III flees.

1212 A Spanish victory at Las
Navas de Tolosa marks the
start of the collapse of the
Almohad dynasty.

1215 The
Dominicans, an order
of preaching monks,
is established.

1219 Forces of the
Fifth Crusade make
gains in Egypt, but fail
to capture Cairo.

The Black Death

The Black Death swept Europe in the fourteenth century.
Between 1347 and 1352, the plague killed about one-third
of the total population and caused great social changes.

Skulls and bones of plague victims were piled up in charnel houses—"bone houses"—around Europe. →

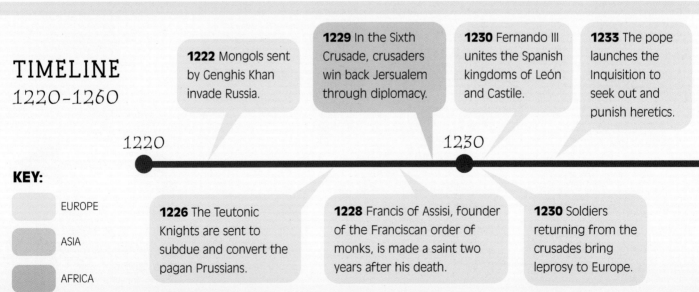

TIMELINE
1220–1260

1222 Mongols sent by Genghis Khan invade Russia.

1229 In the Sixth Crusade, crusaders win back Jersualem through diplomacy.

1230 Fernando III unites the Spanish kingdoms of León and Castile.

1233 The pope launches the Inquisition to seek out and punish heretics.

1220

1230

KEY:

EUROPE

ASIA

AFRICA

1226 The Teutonic Knights are sent to subdue and convert the pagan Prussians.

1228 Francis of Assisi, founder of the Franciscan order of monks, is made a saint two years after his death.

1230 Soldiers returning from the crusades bring leprosy to Europe.

The Black Death originated in Central Asia in the early 1340s and spread along trade routes to the Black Sea, from where Genoese merchant ships transported it to Europe. In just four years it spread throughout the continent, claiming an estimated 20 million lives. In some cities, it was said, there were not enough survivors to bury the dead.

The Disease and Its Cause

The disease struck in three different forms. Bubonic plague, which was spread by contact with an infected person, affected the lymph glands. It caused painful black swellings—"buboes"—in the neck, armpits, and groin. About 75 percent of its victims died, most within a week. Septicemic plague infected the blood, while pneumonic plague, an airborne form, attacked the lungs; it killed more than 90 percent of its victims within three days.

It would be another 500 years before scientists identified the cause of the Black Death as *Yersinia pestis*, a bacterium transmitted to humans by fleas carried on rats. Fourteenth-century scholars attributed the disease to causes

Timeline of the Black Death

c.1341 The Black Death starts in Central Asia.

1345 The plague reaches the Balkans and Black Sea ports.

1347 Genoese merchant ships carry the plague to Sicily, Venice, and Genoa.

1348 The Black Death penetrates western Europe, crossing the English Channel from France into southern England.

1349 The plague spreads into Scotland, the Low Countries, and Scandinavia.

1349 Jews are persecuted in Germany and the Low Countries for causing plague.

1350 By July the plague has gone from most of Europe.

← The Black Death left barely enough people alive to bury the dead.

1242 Alexander Nevsky of Novgorod defeats the Teutonic Knights at the Battle of Lake Peipus.

1250 The Turkish Mameluke dynasty takes power in Egypt.

1258 In the Treaty of Paris, Henry III of England swears loyalty to Louis IX of France.

1250

1260

1244 Muslims reconquer Jerusalem.

1252 Pope Innocent IV authorizes the use of torture on heretics.

1260 At Montaperti, the Ghibillines (supporters of the Holy Roman Emperor) defeat the Guelphs, who support the papacy.

The Black Death followed trade routes from Central Asia to Europe and then moved north and west. ⇒

Timeline (continued)

1351 The plague reaches Russia. England's Parliament fixes wages at pre-plague levels.

1361 The Black Death reappears briefly in England.

1381 Resentment in England over fixed wages and the Poll Tax (introduced in 1380) erupts in the Peasants' Revolt. After initial successes, the rising fails and its leaders are executed.

1400 Europe's population is thought to be around 50 percent lower than it was 100 years earlier.

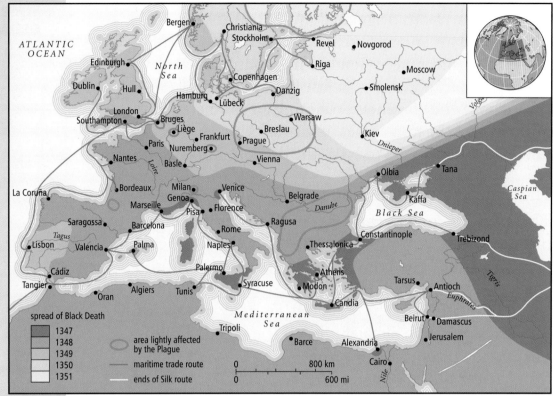

ranging from foul vapors released by earthquakes to the arrangement of the planets. The church, meanwhile, said that the plague was sent to punish humans for their wicked and sinful ways.

The only way to stop the spread of the plague was quarantine. The death toll in Milan was lower than in other cities, for example, probably because any house struck by plague was instantly walled up, entombing sick and healthy occupants alike.

TIMELINE
1260–1300

1262 Byzantine emperor Michael VIII Palaeologus takes Constantinople back from the Latins (crusaders) after 58 years.

1264 Simon de Monfort leads a nobles' revolt against Henry III of England; it is defeated in 1265.

1276 Edward I of England begins an eight-year campaign to subdue the Welsh.

1260

1270

KEY:

EUROPE

ASIA

AFRICA

1260 A Mameluke army halts the Mongol advance at Ayn Jalut in Palestine.

1268 Mamelukes capture the cities of Beirut, Jaffa, and Antioch from their Christian rulers.

Faced with the threat of imminent death, Europeans reacted in often extreme ways. Parents abandoned their dying children and priests refused to hear deathbed confessions. At one Paris hospital, however, nuns nursed strangers until they, too, were struck down. While many citizens turned to prayer and repentance, others resolved to enjoy themselves while they could.

Lasting Effects

The plague had lasting social and economic effects. So many priests died that the Catholic Church had to ordain unsuitable replacements. Their lack of piety made many people disillusioned with established religion. Labor became so scarce that workers could get wages three times higher than they had earned before the plague struck. In England, laws required laborers to work for the same pay as in 1347; these and other harsh measures stoked up anger that would ignite in the Peasants' Revolt of 1381.

Flagellants reenacted the whipping of Jesus at his crucifixion. →

The Flagellants

A flagellant movement began in Germany. People whipped themselves to reenact the scourging of Christ and to atone for the wickedness they blamed for the plague. In 1349, the flagellants turned on the Jews for causing plague. Within a year, they had wiped out most Jews in Germany and the Low Countries. Alarmed at the lawlessness, the Church and local rulers banned the flagellants, executing their leaders.

1281 Osman (Uthman) begins building power in eastern Asia Minor; he founds what will become the Ottoman dynasty.

1290 Edward I expels the Jews from England.

1294 France and England go to war over Gascony.

1297 William Wallace ("Braveheart") begins a Scottish revolt against English rule.

1290

1300

1282 Sicilians revolt against the rule of the French Angevin dynasty.

1287 Alfonso III of Aragón grants important powers to his nobles.

1291 Acre, the last Latin kingdom in West Asia, falls to the Mamelukes.

1298 The English defeat the Scots in the Battle of Falkirk, the beginning of the end for Wallace's revolt.

Glossary

archaeologist Someone who excavates historical sites in search of physical evidence of earlier human activity.

barbarian A member of a tribal society. The word was used by Roman and Byzantine writers to describe any culture they viewed as technologically or culturally inferior.

castle A heavily fortified stronghold, usually built to guard a strategically significant location.

cavalry Soldiers that fight while mounted on horseback.

chivalry A code of conduct associated with knights in poems and songs. It is not known to what extent it was ever followed by knights in practice.

coronation The ceremony of crowning a king, queen, emperor, or empress.

Greek fire A weapon developed in Byzantium during the middle ages that used a jet of sticky, burning liquid to destroy enemy ships.

heretic A person who suggests or propagates a radically altered version of an established belief system.

jousting A competition between armored, mounted warriors that was common in the middle ages. Such competitions usually involved mounted mock-combat with lances.

Orthodox Christianity The Christian denomination that separated from the Catholic Church during the Byzantine period.

peasants' revolt A large-scale rebellion that took place in England in the 14th century. It was started by workers who were angry at attempts to restrict their wages after the Black Death had drastically reduced the population.

plague A term used to describe any of a number of different pandemic diseases that affected Europe and the Near East in the middle ages.

vassal A knight or nobleman who agrees to fight or raise an army for his lord in exchange for being granted ownership of an area of land.

Further Reading

Books

Anderson, Mercedes Padrino. *Feudalism and Village Life in the Middle Ages.* Milwaukee, WI: Gareth Stevens Publishing, 2005.

Bhote, Tehmina. *Charlemagne: The Life and Times of an Early Medieval Emperor.* New York: Rosen Publishing Group, 2004.

Cantor, Norman. *In the Wake of the Plague: The Black Death and the World It Made.* New York: Harper Perennial, 2002.

Corbishley, Mike. *The Middle Ages.* (Cultural Atlas for Young People). New York: Chelsea House Publications, 2007.

Corrick, James A. *The Byzantine Empire.* (World History Series). Detroit, MI: Lucent Books, 2006.

Criswell, David. *Rise of the Holy Roman Empire.* Frederick, MD: Publish America, 2005.

Crouch, David. *The Normans: The History of a Dynasty.* London: Hambledon & London, 2006.

Davenport, John. *The Age of Feudalism.* Detroit, MI: Lucent Books, 2007.

Graham-Campbell, James. *Viking World.* London: Frances Lincoln, 2006.

Hall, Richard. *The World of the Vikings.* New York: Thames & Hudson, 2007.

Hazen, Walter A. *Everyday Life: Middle Ages.* Tuscon, AZ: Good Year Books, 2005.

Heer, Friedrich. *Holy Roman Empire.* London: Phoenix Press, 2002.

Marston, Elsa. *The Byzantine Empire.* New York: Marshall Cavendish Children's Books, 2002.

Martin, Janet. *Medieval Russia, 980-1584.* New York: Cambridge University Press, 2008.

Web Sites

www.chicousd.org/libraries/ elementary/medieval.html
Links to sites offering a taste of life in the Middle Ages

www.middle-ages.org.uk/
Offers quick answers to any question concerning the Middle Ages

www.eyewitnesstohistory.com/ mefrm.htm
Eyewitness accounts of events occurring during the Middle Ages

Index